PLEASE DO NOT TOUCH THIS EXHIBIT

Other books by Jen Campbell

JEN CAMPBELL

PLEASE DO NOT TOUCH
THIS EXHIBIT

BLOODAXE BOOKS

ISBN: 978 1 78037 661 5

First published 2023 by
Bloodaxe Books Ltd,
Eastburn,
South Park,
Hexham,
Northumberland NE46 1BS.

www.bloodaxebooks.com
For further information about Bloodaxe titles
please visit our website and join our mailing list
or write to the above address for a catalogue.

Supported using public funding by
**ARTS COUNCIL
ENGLAND**

Cover design: Neil Astley & Pamela Robertson-Pearce

Printed in Great Britain by Bell & Bain Limited, Glasgow, Scotland, on
acid-free paper sourced from mills with FSC chain of custody certification.

with thanks to Kate
and all the good medics

That's what winter is: an exercise in remembering how to still yourself then how to come pliantly back to life again. An exercise in adapting yourself to whatever frozen or molten state it brings you.

ALI SMITH, *Winter*

ACKNOWLEDGEMENTS

'Anatomy of the Sea' was published in 'Water' issue of *Cunning Folk* magazine. 'First Thing, I Am a Forest' was published in 'Earth' issue of *Cunning Folk* magazine. 'Alopecia' was first runner up in *Poetry London* competition 2022. 'Fell' was highly commended in *Magma* poetry competition 2022. 'The Hospital Is Not a Place for Bodies' was published in *Poetry London*, Spring 2023. 'The Hospital Is Not My House' won 1st prize in *Spelt Magazine* 2022 poetry competition. 'Technical Rehearsal' won 1st prize in the *Sentinel Literary Quarterly* poetry competition. Other poems were published in *Five Dials*.

'This Is Just to Say' was inspired by William Carlos Williams' poem of the same name. 'Trying to Gain Entry into The Republic of Motherhood' was inspired by Liz Berry's poem 'The Republic of Motherhood'.

CONTENTS

At First, the House Is Blue

I don't think I need to explain
that it is winter as I approach the house.

The blue curtains don't just cover
the windows, they also curtain the grass.

The lawn leaks. It's waterlogged felt,
and walking across it is licking

velvet. I wouldn't recommend it, but
it is the only way to reach the house –

this house with its blue door and its blue
brain, which (if I had to) I would draw

as a sea of traffic lights – or perhaps
as some kind of whale.

Anatomy of the Sea

After the nuclear disaster of Chernobyl in April 1986,
radioactive rain fell across Europe. In the following three
years, in the northeast of England, there were many more
cases of children born with limb differences. I was born in
January 1987, in Sunderland, with Ectrodactyly Ectodermal
Dysplasia Clefting Syndrome

I

The rain falls in northern England and still
the women dig deeper for their children.

They rip fingertips below the green
houses. Bellow in the soil and marvel

at the wet, wet earth so much like the sea –
of which they are afraid. Not mother

earth. Not the bearer or the ark. Nor
the trees. No, they search the soil for seeds

and they are thankful. They are grateful.
It's only after that my mother is grave.

II

Nine months later, I am clawed
from the sea.

A river child.

A lobster baby.

Oh, they say. *Oh*.
All fingers and thumbs.

My blanket: petrichor,
and we drown in genetics.

III

Late at night, my friends and I are watching
The Hills Have Eyes and I know that I am

the only body horrified.

They dare each other to run outside
but I stay put.

My meat heart pounding –

Monster. Monster. Monstrous.

IV

In an Airbnb in Copenhagen
my husband and I watch
the TV show *Chernobyl.*

Jared Harris and Emily Watson
are saving the world but –
its people are burning, and

I have rage, the likes of which you
would not believe.

The April before I arrived,
men were godlike in their mistakes.

Obsessed with their creations.

Now my hands are   birds
                                    elephants
                                    rock salt
                                    constellations
                                    anemone.

Listen to me:
until the 1800s, anyone
with a disfigurement
was medically called a monster.

    V

Somewhere, I am certain
Mary Shelley stands on a mountain top,
commanding the clouds.

It has stormed for weeks, and she
is lost for words – haunted

by images of a jigsawed man.

We all look skywards.
Seawards.

See the tumbling birds, feel
the damp soil inking into our feet.

This is where we were meant to meet.

We mother-hunt for hours in the flesh of the earth.
We plant ourselves, firmly

and cross our numbered digits. Then, *oh* then –
we summon the rain.

Dear [_____], I would be grateful for your opinion on this deformed baby girl (no name yet). She has a deranged skeleton and I suspect will need surgery asap. No doubt she will be of particular interest to [_____] in genetics. Will refer.

Dear [_____], Thank you for referring this young lass, with severe congenital deformities. Interesting indeed! Suspect larger syndrome at play. Lobster claw present etc. Will schedule first operation for twelve weeks. Unable to map tendons. X-ray proved unhelpful at this very early stage.

The Hospital Is Not My House

I

The hospital is not a place for geography. The girl swims out of the x-ray machine and climbs into the Colosseum, by which we mean the proscenium, by which we mean the operating theatre. The blue magicians roll up their sleeves and plant trees to decide where her body should be. A sapling here, a root pulled there. They label all her countries, lick a paint brush across the borders, hire Victorian seamstresses to cover the skin where her colours don't match. Their act requires a metal pole they stole from a sailing ship, and this they shove beneath her skin and motorise. They blow a whistle and her bones dance. Her hip is now her palm, is now a web, is now a waltz. They puppet-sew by hand – stand and tuck the girl inside an orange boat. As the curtain falls, they propel her into deeper waters, with the lions and the warriors, clean forgetting she is still sound asleep.

II

The hospital is not a place for literature. The lights are out and the young girl tiptoes to the edge of a tree, by which we mean the edge of a bed. By which we mean the edge of a corridor, where she is searching for the bathroom. The bathroom being the wet field that half-hides the moon. Half-asleep, the girl questions how she can hold the moon when she cannot hold anything. When she is grafted to herself and to this building. When her new skin slips, for she is wearing. She is wearing satin pyjamas to stop the stitches catching. She is wearing satin pyjamas to be a fish, and her hips are now part of her hands, and the forest grips her feet. The trees have her, as the bedsheets flash the light from the sea to help her find her way back along the pebbled ward. She finds the moon for a moment, hovering gently above the sink, a giant rock pool, or a swollen mother, and she allows the current to pull her swiftly back to bed.

III

The hospital is not a place for mathematics. The physio-therapist asks the girl whether she would prefer her hands to be wrapped in blue seaweed or pink. The seaweed sets when she's asleep. It concretes itself and pulses so that her palms swell up, two puffer fish. They itch, itch, itch, which (they say) is only to be expected. The doctors instruct the girl to wear these splints and build a castle. They give her building blocks shaped like gums. They step back behind their glass with their clipboards and their eyebrows, and they proceed to comment on her geometry. They say each half of her body must swim in synchronicity. They squint and shake their heads and declare that she is a series of triangles. All pointed bones and lobster claws. The seaweed clamps her hands to stop her catching words that float around the room – stop her from being catching, too. The doctors pat her waxen head, wash their hands, and send her home.

Dear [_____], For your records, this three-year-old was admitted under the care of [____] for further surgery to her right hand; this being her thirteenth operation to date. We have grown fond of her. Recent biopsy shows fibrosis. Excuse the pun but she knows this ward like the back of her hand!

Dear [_____], Jennifer has a crooked skeleton but is very active and eager to please – a fascinating specimen. Nerve blocks administered. Eye surgery scheduled. She likes cornflakes, milk and water. Likes fruit and cheese. Capillary return three seconds, pink and warm.

The Hospital Is Not a Place for Bodies

I

The hospital is not a place for biology. The girl is asked
to choose a set of eyes from a bed of irises. She blinks
through the iodine, knowing that this is back-to-front
because, of course, she cannot see them. Instead of
choosing with her hands (she is wary of bursting them
like bath pearls), she speaks to the eyes directly. She
locates their little ear drums and manages to charm them.
She requests they travel with her down the rivulets, and
the three of them paddle out of the hospital garden.
Doctors call the girl a pirate, give her a ship that she
suspects is just a billet – but at least she can pretend
these sheets are sails, that saline seawater. And though
the mattress may be waterlogged, she is familiar with this
vertigo: her webbed flamingo skeleton tilting on its young
sea legs.

II

The hospital is not a place for languages. When the girl has half-grown, the magicians cut open her skull to excavate her shark teeth. Teeth that have swum up to her cheek bones and wrapped themselves in sinew. The archaeologists anchor them with silver hooks and latch them onto pulleys. They give the girl a metal mouth. Her lips part to reveal a pirate ship. The men hold a mirror and she struggles to speak, remembering a ghost story about a creature whose mouth opened so wide it swallowed the sea. She watches as her salt tongue slow-grows barnacles. The men tighten the ropes, hoping pearls will avalanche down her face. They wait, but nothing moves, and so – the magicians open and close her puppet mouth. The archaeologists admire their craftsmanship. Both ask the shark-girl to grin, then swim away.

III

The hospital is not a place for history. When the grown-girl visits the medical museum, she is all awash with skeletons. Bodies hauled in by doctors, hung up like brittle carpets. She gapes at the way their bones bow – so many shapes, so many ships. She slips their names inside her brain and walks with them for company. Now, when far-flung doctors come to town and ask her for a show, she lets them stroke her sewn-on skin, half-listening to shanties. She half-drowns, and they applaud. After-wards, they name her a good little sea creature. They wind her up mechanically. Marvel at how her brined eyes blink. At how she's mostly starfish.

Dear [_____], Jennifer was very anxious upon admission today. She haemorrhaged post-surgery and was put in the recovery position until fully conscious. We have now exhumed more excess bone. The web is drying out well, but her mouth still needs seeing to. Interestingly, she has a younger sister who is completely normal.

Dear [_____], This afternoon, Jennifer's defects were sutured with Z plasties. Once again, Wolfe skin grafts were inserted into the base of her fingers – this time the donor site was her left leg. She seems to be able to walk fine. This being her fourth general anaesthetic in six weeks, I suggest a pause of further procedures, as her next eye surgery is also due in the summer. Next year, she will be starting school.

For a While, the House Is Green

So green I think I might be able
to eat it.

So green I guess a giant
may have a hand in it.

Green teeth in the window boxes.
Green smoke from the chimney.

Then beneath the stretch of lawn,
the flesh composting down.

The House of Mirrors Is Owned by the Freak Show

At the Victorian open-air museum, there's
a hall of glass, a historic lake that takes
the sewn-on parts of you and throws them
into an evening show. And if those mirrors
happen to know that parts of you were once
an animal, you had better sprint (fast!) to
the carousel and pray those horses can run
like hell – you: sea-fearing little Lobster Girl.

The Body Festival

The carnival is here. You eat
it up like candy floss.

In the fairground, apples
are sticking to the grasses

and lasses are in the body
tank, expanding and/or

drowning, fireworks
plaited into strawberry hair.

Your bodies have eyes
the colour of gills.

The ground is littered
with misplaced feet.

Our hearts are ruby in the trees.

The dead are walking – fishing.
They are coming up for air.

Ghost-whisperer

The ghosts chew on the ends of our Sunday shoes. Mam says pins and needles is where The Spirits are passing through. We have never made the dead bite this strong before. The table is set; in the middle are the blackberries I spent the morning picking. They've turned all funny, and my fingernails are squid ink now – little gravestones, pearly dead. Don't annoy them, Mam says, pushing me forward. I have to squeeze past Grandma's chair, take one step, then another. Someone giggles, mostly terrified. Dad sneezes, 'cause he's allergic. In the centre of the room, I check my dress for creases. Them what can't breathe like things smooth. They wish the world was flat, so their souls don't fall off the curve; so they can cling to time like limpets. Mam says you've got to empty yourself, else it won't work – so I imagine pouring myself into ponds from a rotting jam jar. My face in the water, panicked, like it ain't sure how it got there. I picture myself as fishes, the type that are see-through – where you can see all their innards swimming around. I can feel my heart pulsing in all its translucent glory. Their hands have it now, lots of 'em, all sandpaper and prunes. They grab at my hair, too – invisibly twist it. They're whisperin' in bubbles, brewing sacrilege. I point my feet out sideways, hold my breath, and listen.

Sometimes, the House Is Made of Glass

When I am feeling
anchored, I hunt

for the
translucent house.

It has to be
a cloudy day

or else the light
will frame me.

The house flickers
into focus,

jellyfish, then
gone again.

Its rooms are
blown sea

glass, floating
in the soil.

Dear [_____], Following on from renal complications and jaw surgery, Jennifer is making good process. Did you know she now plays the piano? It is quite extraordinary. Next month [_____] is visiting from America. I wondered if we could arrange a viewing for him, as Jennifer is the first of her kind on our list.

Please Do Not Touch This Exhibit

At the back of the museum, I meet a man
who tells me in no uncertain terms that
he collects the tongues of storytellers.

His own tongue quivers in his cheeks.
He licks his lips in doublespeak and yet
he summons me to his home. There:

he shows me heaving shelves, chock
full of carved out books – their grooves
used to store his brood of salted tongues. Still,

such pressing words — and all that I can hear
are horses running from his mouth, those spiders
in the walls, these wallflowers in my hand.

Technical Rehearsal

You know, sir, there are bones in my body
that are yet to have names. Terrifying
elevators, pulling me up.

I am all of this, ballooned.
Rooms filled up with furniture that is
not my own, rented out to cherry trees.

Together we are plays that will go wrong. Sir,
I am uncertain in the seasick theatre,
counting all of my rooms.

I am a house, sir. A picture of a house.
I am a house, sir. A house with birds.

First Thing, I Am a Forest

When I wake up and I cannot see, I reach
for the hyaluronic acid on my bedside

table – hoping that I do not accident-
ally knock it floorwards, hear it

roll beneath the bedframe, on and on
into the graveyard of a spider-queen.

See, there are webs stuck to my eyelids,
too; sewn shut to keep the ghosts out of this

temporary bone house. I've begun to wear
a rain jacket in an attempt to escape

this weathering. Like an owl might
hold an umbrella, or a tree might

fold itself inside a greenhouse:
an origami giantess. And I guess

that when I wake up and I cannot see,
I imagine that our mattress is the earth of some

far-flung kingdom – one where, good god,
it is rude to stand and stare, and so everyone there

just pretends they are a tree. How wild,
this ancient forestry. How bone dry,

                I blink

to let the rain in; wait
to see   a somewhat scratched-out sky.

Dear [_____], As Jennifer approaches adulthood, I recommend care at Rare Diseases alongside her other hospital admissions. She is also now experiencing scarring (permanent) alopecia, and perhaps a wig would be helpful in the long run? Certainly, a perplexing syndrome. I wish her well!

Alopecia

I

The first creature that falls from my head
is a hedgehog. I stand still
in the shower and hold it –

                then drown it.

All pins and needles. No nature
photographer, I spill out
of the shower and hurl it
into the toilet.

                I flush it,

just my animal
heart remaining.

II

For some time, I think
I dreamed it

                – but

then the animals
begin to breed.

They shed across my pillow,
undress on every jumper, scatter

34

naked when the lights dim
and their skin becomes balloons:

> a field mouse, a hamster,
> a stoat – tiptoe across
> my throat and
> lick my scarecrow scalp.

III

Before long, I am a petting zoo.

I would say that I mind
but I know that pity is awful

and so, I carry treats in my dresses
and I learn to whistle beast-song.

IV

If I close my eyes and
brush my hair, I swear

I can hear the
accidental animals
falling out of me:

> a nightjar
> an owl
> a woodpecker
> a lark.

V

These days I own
more hats than pets.

        Two dozen
        tiny nests, perched
        above my wardrobe

and me: a magician,
        a conjurer   peering at a mirror.

All wide-eyed in this ark.

My Brain Is a Sleeping Thing

I find it hanging on a tree branch, tied
loosely with gold ribbon from some past
Christmas. You know, the glittery kind

that feels horrible to touch. The kind you keep
because you think you'll use it to wrap up someone
else's gift. Now, it's cushioning my brain

and it scratches. I notice the other trees
are holding normal things; things you'd gladly
put inside your mouth. I stretch up

to touch my brain and
my fingers don't quite reach it.

Vaguely, I think I should try to find someone
to ask about the harvest – but my tinsel brain
is busy, farming nasty little things.

We Must Admit, the House Is Pink

In fact, it is a fleshy-peachy-stitched-up bouncy castle.
We are aware that the adverts in the catalogue may
have been misleading. We hope you know that on any other
day we would invite you in for revelations, but we appear
to have misplaced the front door, and all the windows are
now shuttered, closed. We are deeply embarrassed about
this loss of control; we hope to find you another home.

Fell

When my hair became feral and abandoned
my head, I remembered the foxes at the end

of our road. How their orange fur tumbled like
scarves in the wash. How the youngest one waited

at the edge of the wood – a four-legged
ghost who would perch in the sun. Or a bird

tossing feathers right out of its nest. Now men
draw a square on the back of my head. I feel

the skeleton skin with the tips of my hands.
Think a song for the leaves that are falling.

For Some Reason, I Can't Stop
Writing About Lighthouses

I turn on the bedside light and the walls
slip sideways. Besides, the lamppost
outside our window is some kind
of wraith. Also, I was sure there was
a track by Dustin O'Halloran
called *Lighthouse*, but when I went
to check I realised it's actually
called *We Move Lightly* – which happens to be
the opposite of how I feel right now. Apart
from wading through something dark
and complicated, I have now committed
the cardinal sin of mentioning something
which you cannot hear – unless
you grab a bow and arrow and go hunt it down.
But it is cold, and the tide is out, so let me
describe the music simply as a
barnacled piano. Bloated, light-footed,
full of underwater chords. I guess
now we have to wait for the linguists
to arrive. They'll be thirsty in their wetsuits,
carrying their sonar gear; busy
calculating the gap between the thing I am
describing and the words I just grasped at.
It's so hard to put words to anything.
The light of the kettle flickers. There's a boat
crawling across the kitchen. Here they come,
in the green dawn. I stall and offer them
a cup of peppermint tea. After all, it's not time
to put the big lights on. Not when the forecast
is hovering, and there's an orb above the rocks.

In My Dream, the House Is Dark

This could be because my eyes are closed
but (more likely) it is because the house is
now an x-ray. The house has taken to watching
films about deep-sea fish – those who have
their insides out, and has realised it needs
to show me its precious wooden skeleton.
It uses oil lamps to highlight areas where
particular care is needed, then does
a silly dance to take the edge off the haunted
feeling. So as not to seem rude, I hum along
to the familiar tune and try not to wake up
until the house has decided it has done enough
and settles on its haunches, its carcass fizzing in the dark.

When I Revisit This Room, I Want to Leave Again

While she waits for the computer to restart, she gently
bites the end of her biro.

The screen flickers, then it dies. She sighs:

> 'You could just get pregnant, then have an abortion.'

I nearly snap in my seat; marvelling at what
an awful magician this one is – just brazenly

pulling blood from a hat. She taps
at the keys, not looking at me:

> 'So, Jennifer, have you thought about that?'

Have I thought about it?

Perhaps she would like a tour of my brain
where I store the faces of every child I'll never have?

> 'That is cheaper for us than IVF, you see.'

> > [My geneticist is on holiday, so instead of
> > talking to him, I am talking to a woman whose
> > name I have since banished. A doctor who has
> > somehow managed to distance herself from her
> > disabled patients to such a degree that I am
> > not sure that I exist, let alone my hypothetical
> > children.]

She goes on to explain how easy it would be,
just a scan, just to peek – and if it looked like me:

> 'A quick procedure, all gone.'

42

She stifles a yawn, ignoring
the copies of me that now litter her floor.

> [There is a student doctor sitting in on our
> session. He is a fluster of embarrassed feathers.
> 'I'm so sorry,' he mouths, clearly, behind her
> back.
>
> What a fragment of humanity.]

I struggle to explain why her suggestion is not
the same as us gathering eggs and putting them beneath

a microscope. I say I couldn't cope, personally,
actually – emphatically not... but she has already

glazed over, disappointed by my lack
of sacrifice. For who am I

to deny a magician
their great act of disappearance?

> [She tuts, angrily sifting through my file. After
> a while, says I'll be pleased to hear that, even
> though IVF is more expensive than me having
> a hypothetical abortion (should my hypothetical
> child, in fact fifty percent of my hypothetical
> children, deign to be born the same as me), it
> is still much cheaper than me having a child
> with my syndrome, because of all the operations
> that child would then need.
>
> Therefore, she concludes, I can have my IVF,
> if it will stop me from reproducing myself.]

'That way, we still save money, you see.'

In disbelief, I sense that this is the part
where I am supposed to applaud.

Somehow, I am able to pick up
my phantom limbs, and I clap for her.

I clap, and clap, and clap,
until my wrists are raw.

Until I'm pretty sure   I still exist.

Poem as Bad Doctor

Please imagine
that this poem is
not talking to you
but is instead
talking to the
person sitting
next to you, who
happens to be
present but is not
actually the
subject of this
poem. Scuttle to
the right, then
merge into the
margins and wait
to be told when
this poem, this
poem that is not
your poem, this
body of text, is
going to end. And
when the words
cease, please wait
to be told how
you're supposed
to take them.
How on earth
you're supposed
to swallow them
down.

Somehow, the House Is Orange

The neighbours believe that the house is trying
to get attention by turning itself into a volcano.
Its windows have been remade from candlewax
which means that, in all its Christingled glory,
the house is melting or merely crying. A local
artist has been commissioned to paint the house
in its current state. There are rumours that tigers
are sleeping in the basement but the artist is sweating
too much to get close enough to check. Later,
they will tell anyone who will listen that they could
definitely hear a roaring – the clatter of rooms
yawning – when their drawings went up in flames.

The Five Stages of IVF

The boy stands in our garden
holding all of the snow.
He can't be a snowman,
I insist. He is far too young
for frostbite. He might
be mythic. Or prophetic.
Did anyone see him arrive?

The snowboy's eyes are
kingfishers. Blazing countries
we would like to visit.
Behind him a
squirrel is stealing
all of the food. Bending
over backwards – winter
olympics. The young boy does not
blink, cradling his snow globe.

The whole world is a blizzard.

We refuse to talk of snow
babies incubating in fables.
How their fingerprints
are the scattered names
of endangered species.
Instead, we dip our palms
in icing sugar and press
our mouths to the window.

Our longings skitter
around the kitchen
like so much white noise.

When It Arrives, It Weighs 5kg

I fill out the form to request my childhood
medical notes. In many ways, it's like

I'm inviting myself to dinner. I think
of those apps that tell you what type of fruit

your shapeshifting foetus is. I grab a pen
and make up my own key. I work out how tall

my medical folder will be in bread slices. Calculate
how much kneaded skin will tumble from

the envelope. I sandwich myself between the kitchen
and the letterbox, waiting for myself to arrive.

The Hospital Is Not Big Enough for the Two of Us

I

The hospital is not a place for nostalgia. The woman is advised it probably would be wise to leave her younger self outside. They hand her a knife, ask her if she knows how to use it, say it's quite expensive and – 'judging by the state of [her] hands' – they hope she'll try very hard not to drop it. If she doesn't feel comfortable making the separation, they can always do it for her. Not a problem. Just ask. And if it isn't too crass, can she leave the severed child in the car park? It's fine, they find they don't usually mind; most of them enjoy the weather and the people watching. Not to worry. Could you hurry? We don't want to get caught in the rain –

II

The hospital is not a place for remembering. The woman ignores their advice and (when they're not looking) she puts her younger self inside her pocket. The smell of the hospital makes her younger self vomit, and although the woman has not been to this specific hospital before, she feels she knows it like the back of her hand (no pun intended). The visitors snake up the stairs and the wings spread out in all directions. The hospital is a pterodactyl, its walls will not stand still; and until the woman can get access to the proto-mothers and the dinosaur nests, she is told to try to be less stressed. Her younger self peers over the edge of the pocket, ready to do a dance for anyone who needs to see it. She stares up at the woman and asks her what sort of dance she should do: a red one, a blue one, a green one or –

III

The hospital is not a place for colours. The woman tries to comfort her younger self with poster paints but neither of them can reach the walls to draw on. The floor is waxy underfoot, the corridor a candle, and the woman can't handle how fast the magicians are spelling. Something about freezing and thawing and how there's no way of knowing whether the doors either side of them are going to spit them back out. The younger self begins to chant, stuck in a series of rememberings. The magicians tick some squares and cross some others, usher them into an off-white room, where the prehistoric sounds are muffled and a kind woman offers to cradle the younger self, just to take the weight off, just so the woman can enter the next room safely. Just so –

Trying to Gain Entry into The Republic of Motherhood

(after Liz Berry)

I asked to cross the border into the Republic of Motherhood
and found myself in a waiting room, an overgrown waiting room.
When my name was called, I took off my clothes and I let them
scan me – knowing these borrowed instruments were used
by the already-mothers, searching the waters for their seal-like
babes. I removed my wig and shuffled down their bed. They parted
my legs, relaying their instructions, then sent me to work
on the Farmland of Motherhood. I stabbed myself twice daily,
injecting resilience, collecting purple-blue badges as prizes
to claim access to the Republic of Motherhood. My body bloomed,
turned itself into a chicken, my heartbeat going boomboomboom
as drugs spooled through the factory of my body. I mentally
decorated our home to make room for us all. As required,
every week I sat with my sisters in the passport office at
the Department of Motherhood. None of us looked sideways
but all of us loved each other. Surely, I thought, I would die
for these women and their carefully chosen leggings; I would die
for their frantic calendars and their nervous laughter – and if
I could, I would stamp every single visa, cry out
that we should storm the royal banquet (to which we had not
yet been invited), and stuff ourselves with riches before
declaring our corridor a part of their country. But no.
No, that is not what we did. We patiently queued, then we
got back to work; cherry angiomas freckling our skin.
Our bloated bellies hungry, so hungry, they rumbled all shift long.

This Is Just to Say

(after William Carlos Williams)

I have swallowed
the poems
that spoke of
pandemics

and which
you were probably
hoping
to snack on

Forgive me
I can't traverse them
like streets
in shielded snow.

When I Go to the Woods

It's mostly to touch the moss-covered
cities. It's in the hope I don't slip
on the oak tongue; on those wriggling
dragons that course fog into the dawn.
And when I go into the woods, it's not
because I'm exiting my body. Hell,
my skin is not a mackintosh, and I don't
leave myself behind. Besides, we cannot
change this noise – now the starlings
are new sirens. Yes, rows of little mimics:
choirs of puffed-up, rained-on players.
That's why this morning the woods are heavy
with the sound of many ambulances. The petrol
bird-made trill of a claustrophobic field.
Oh, what a mirrored world this is
for us to stumble into – emergency
on every side, cushioned by the leaves.

The Weekend the Garden Reflected Our House

My husband cut the ivy and was horrified to discover a bird's nest –

unwrapped and brash exposed. Inside, two eggs: perched.

'I think they're hollow,' he said, his ear tilted towards the twigs.

Those little spooks said nothing, blue by cold or just by breed.

'I think they're empty,' he said. But, still, he placed leaves around them.

We swept the wet sky for their mother, weather guiltily seeping in.

The Trees Are Part of the Process

It seems so predictable
that I grew these
eggs in springtime.
That we let them
rest over the summer
as farmers peered
beneath their skins.

Then, naturally:
in the orange months,
when only one
of them remained,
we let them place it
         (gently)
inside my womb.

Of course, we waited – for two
weeks made of Sundays but

I don't know what
to tell you, except:
the autumn leaves
are dying, and we
cannot stop them
spiralling, cannot stop
them entering, cannot
prevent their fall.

Now, the House Is Red

But it's not the kind of red that you
would notice from the road. Instead

the red comes from a light
in the hall, a limpet on the ceiling.

The windows are breathed on, so it's
impossible to tell if the lightbulb is red or if

it's just the lampshade. Either way the organs,
the furniture, the god-damn water supply

are telling the house it is red today. All the lights
pulse red, first velour then less so. I have the urge

to colour match this shade – to take a swatch
to the hardware store and ask them, beg them,

for the name of this colour, the name of this red
(red cotton, red glass), but I know if I asked

they would search through their ledger
where it was never written down.

This Doesn't Have a Name Yet

I have nowhere left to fit this
sadness. Now that I have
birthed it, it insists on running
around – all naked and vulnerable
and occasionally giggling like a
swimming pool.

I step into the kitchen and
drench myself in it. Its chlorined
aesthetic. And, around the walls,
its grief-soaked tote bags
full of the things that
no one really wants. The stuff
that can't go to charity shops – can't
be left on people's doorsteps,
like I'm the stork of whatever this is:
the Santa Claus of joy
I am forbidden to experience.

So, instead, I tread water.

On Sundays I am the Easter bunny.
Cracking eggs into batter
and slamming the oven door
so hard I hope it breaks.
                              Yet
it doesn't, because for some
reason I cannot explain I am still
so bloody gentle – and this is
hilarious, because (right now)
my anger is staring
at the oven
as if it were the sun.

Some God of Light that I could
bribe with gingerbread or cake.

The House Is All the Colours, All at Once

As a temporary measure, the house puts
in a request to be removed from the market.
I wash its organs in the sink, sweep the phantoms
from the floorboards and spend several days
smothering fires in rooms that should have
remained locked. As I unhook the weather
machine, the house and I spy a fox tugging
at the edge of this painting, here to tip us
into the whatever-next. Its green-tipped
paws knead the garden, delicate teeth peeling back
the wallpaper where (underneath) all the colours run
to meet each other: in a sigh, in a rush, in a roar.

Common Side Effects

Yesterday was the big, good rain.
The one that fills the sinkholes.
The one that ushers you to bed,
saying: I'll wash up. You rest. Now,

yesterday was the good, big rain.
Some blazing onomatopoeia tip-
toeing through the streets. Pausing
every now and then, simply to rip some

one in two. Yes, yesterday: that rain.
The hulk kind, the grand kind.
It kindly flooded all my organs. Left me
shipwrecked, rotten, blessed.

Jen Campbell grew up by the sea in the northeast of England. She is an award-winning poet and bestselling author of twelve books for adults and children. Her most recent titles include *The Beginning of the World in the Middle of the Night*, *The Sister Who Ate Her Brothers*, and *Marceline: Defender of the Sea*. Her books have been translated into over twenty languages. She has won both the Jane Martin Poetry Prize and an Eric Gregory Award.

Her poetry pamphlet *The Hungry Ghost Festival* was published by *The Rialto* in 2012. Her first book-length collection, *The Girl Aquarium*, was published by Bloodaxe Books in 2019. It was shortlisted for the poetry category of the Books Are My Bag Readers Awards 2019 and was a semifinalist for the Goodreads Choice Awards 2019 (Best Poetry category). She won the *Spelt* Poetry Competition 2022 for her poem 'The Hospital Is Not My House' from her second collection, *Please Do Not Touch This Exhibit* (Bloodaxe Books, 2023). She currently lives in London.

Find out more at: www.jen-campbell.co.uk